WORLD WAR II DAY BY DAY

THE THIRD REICH

1923–1945

Charlie Samuels

BROWN BEAR BOOKS

Published by Brown Bear Books Ltd
4877 N. Circulo Bujia
Tucson, AZ 85718
USA

and
First Floor
9-17 St Albans Place
London N1 0NX

© 2013 Brown Bear Books Ltd

ISBN: 978-1-78121–039-0

Library of Congress Cataloging-in-Publication Data
available upon request

Editorial Director: Lindsey Lowe
Managing Editor: Tim Cooke
Design Manager: Keith Davis
Designer: Jerry Udall
Picture Manager: Sophie Mortimer
Children's Publisher: Anne O'Daly
Production Director: Alastair Gourlay

Manufactured in the United States of America

CPSIA compliance information: Batch#: AG/5507

Photographic credits:

Front Cover: Robert Hunt Library.
All photographs Robert Hunt Library except:
Christopher Ailsby Historical Archives: 36b.

Contents

Introduction

The Third Reich—or "third empire"—came into existence on January 30, 1933. It was the creation of the Nationalist Socialist German Workers' Party (NASDAP), also known as the Nazi Party, and of its Führer, or leader, Adolf Hitler. Born in Austria in 1889, Hitler was later rejected by the Academy of Fine Arts in Vienna. The rejection made him highly resentful, particularly of Vienna's Jewish population.

Hitler forms his philosophy

Hitler moved to Munich in 1913 and the following year was an enthusiastic volunteer after the outbreak of World War I. He served in the trenches, where he was decorated for bravery and wounded in action.

Like many other soldiers, Hitler was dismayed by the German surrender and the Weimar Republic created to rule postwar Germany. He and his supporters blamed the politicians for defeat, claiming—with little justification—that the government had betrayed the army at a time when it could have kept fighting.

The country was in turmoil. Its economy was in ruins and while the disbanded soldiers and their officers viewed the republic with distaste, communists and socialists tried to spark a revolution among German workers. To control these revolutionaries, state governments turned to the Freikorps, bands of right-wing former soldiers.

A new party

Hitler, meanwhile, was trained in political intelligence and sent by his superiors to report on the activities of a small group known as the German Workers' Party. The tiny party

As Führer of the Third Reich, Hitler is saluted by the Reichstag, or parliament, in 1941.

was opposed to both the "Jewish conspiracy" it said controlled Europe's economy and to Communism. Such ideas appealed to Hitler, who joined the party and soon took it over, renaming it the National Socialist German Workers' Party. Its growth was helped by the support of Ernst Röhm, chief of staff to the commandant of the Munich military region. He introduced Hitler to influential figures such as General Erich von Ludendorff, a World War I hero and right-wing nationalist.

Hitler gained publicity for the party, staging fights against socialists and communists. Hitler was supported by the Sturmabteilung or SA (Storm Detachment), tough former soldiers who became known as the Brownshirts. In March 1923 he formed what would later become the Schutzstaffel or SS (Defense Squad). This was his elite personal guard, who were as loyal to him as the SA was to Röhm.

Rallying point

Guarded by the SA, Hitler staged a series of mass meetings in Munich. By fall 1923, he had made the Nazi Party a rallying point of opposition to the government in Berlin. As the

Ranks of Brownshirts march in unison past Hitler and Benito Mussolini, during the Italian dictator's visit to Berlin in September 1937.

world economy slumped and German inflation rose uncontrollably, the Weimar Republic became less and less popular.

Hitler planned a putsch, or coup, to seize power from the government in Bavaria. The so-called Beer Hall Putsch began on November 9, 1923, when Hitler maneuvered Ludendorff and other leaders into supporting him. Next day, the Nazis marched into the center of the city, but when they were fired upon by police, they surrendered. The leaders were arrested. Hitler was put on trial. He used the occasion to gain publicity for the Nazis' beliefs—but the failure of the putsch convinced him that he could only achieve power through democratic means.

The Nazis hold their first Party Day in Munich on January 28, 1923.

FEBRUARY 24, 1924, Munich

In Munich, Hitler, Ludendorff and eight co-defendants go on trial for treason after their attempt to seize the local government in a Putsch. The outcome will affect far more than just their own futures. The trial ends on April 1. Hitler is back in prison but he has won the propaganda battle and is a national hero.

APRIL 1924, Germany

Ernst Röhm is given the job of reconstructing the officially still-illegal SA.

MAY 1924, Germany

Although the Nazi Party is outlawed, Nazis stand as the National Socialist Freedom Movement in elections. They win nearly two million votes; 32 of 34 candidates are elected to the Reichstag. In a second election in December, their vote is more than halved.

DECEMBER 20, 1924, Landsberg

While in prison, Hitler dictates a book setting out his political beliefs to Rudolf Hess, who has taken a job as his secretary. The royalties from the book that was later titled *Mein Kampf* ("My Struggle") will become the main source of Hitler's income.

Hitler addresses the officers of the party at a meeting in the mid–1920s.

Treason – a crime intended to weaken or overthrow a government.

FEBRUARY 27, 1925, Munich

The ban on the NSDAP was lifted in January. After his release from prison, Hitler assembles the party faithful in the Bürgerbräukeller in Munich to re-establish the NSDAP.

APRIL 25, Germany

Hitler orders the former member of the *Stosstrupp Adolf Hitler* and his chauffeur, Julius Schreck, to form a new guard unit for Hitler himself. The new headquarters guard is called the *Schutzstaffel* or SS Protection Squad. The new SS initially has just eight members.

JULY 1926, Weimar

At a rally, Hitler hands over the highly prized "Blood Flag" to the SS. This was the swastika flag carried during the 1923 Beer Hall Putsch. The SS units are now the elite units of the SA (Brownshirts) and will bear the Deutschland Erwache standards at meetings and rallies.

NOVEMBER 1, 1926, Germany

Hitler makes Hauptmann Franz Pfeffer von Salomon commander of the SA throughout the whole of the country.

Hitler attends the Nazi Party Day held in Nuremberg in 1927.

AUGUST 1927, Germany

Hitler continues to reveal his *Weltanschauung* (World View). He believes that the Aryan-Nordic race is the founder and preserver of civilization, and the Jewish race its destroyer.

JANUARY 9, 1928, Germany

Hitler appoints Goebbels as the head of propaganda for the whole of the country.

MAY 1928, Berlin

In Reichstag elections, the right-wing drop falls. Nazis win just 810,000 votes. This gives them only 12 out of 491 seats in the Reichstag.

KEY PEOPLE: Heinrich Himmler

Himmler (1900–1945) became the leader of the new SS in January 1929. By 1936 he controlled the German police network. Himmler took over the Gestapo and widened its control. He was the head of the concentration camp system that would kill six million Jews. By 1944, he was also head of the Home Army. A week before Hitler's suicide, Himmler, realizing the war was lost, tried to negotiate Germany's surrender. Furious with Himmler's treachery, Hitler dismissed him from all posts. Captured by the British in May 1945, Himmler took cyanide and was dead within seconds.

Aryan – in Nazi belief, a white member of a Nordic super race.

Members of the SA stage a rally in the town of Meiningen in 1931.

JANUARY 14, 1930, Berlin

Horst Wessel is murdered in Berlin. Wessel had joined the Brownshirts at the age of 19, and had written the lyrics for the celebrated "Horst Wessel Song," which became the official anthem of the Nazis. After his murder, which the Nazis blamed on communists, he became a Nazi symbol of a martyr who had given his life for the Nazi cause.

SEPTEMBER 14, 1930, Berlin

Some 30 million Germans go to the polls in Reichstag elections from which the Nazis emerge as the second-largest party, with 107 seats. The Social Democrats have 143 seats and the Communists have 77 seats. The Nazis have polled 6,409,000 votes.

AUGUST 2–4, 1929, Nuremberg

The Nazi Party convenes its annual rally at Nuremberg. There are 60,000 members and 2,000 members of the Hitler Youth present. Hitler sits and listens as his opening statement is read out to his supporters. The speech rehashes all the themes that have by now become highly familiar, such as the injustice shown to German soldiers by politicians during and after World War I and the unfairness of the Allied-imposed terms of the Treaty of Versailles. As usual, Hitler vehemently attacks communists and the Jews.

JANUARY 15, 1931, Germany

Erich Röhm becomes chief of staff of the SA. He is only answerable to Hitler, the Führer.

APRIL 1931, Germany

Hitler agrees to abide by a government ban on public demonstrations.

KEY PEOPLE: Joseph Goebbels

Joseph Goebbels (1897–1945) was the Nazis' propaganda chief and later Minister of Propaganda. He was against the war in Europe, realizing that Germany would unnecessarily risk losing its position of power. Despite the initial victories of 1940, Goebbels did not think the Nazis should expect a quick or easy victory. He was probably the only Nazi leader to correctly judge the length and horror of the war. Goebbels saw himself as being a general, his ministry as a general staff and the propaganda war as important as any fighting on the front. Goebbels and his wife were in the bunker with Hitler in Berlin in May 1945. He shot himself rather than be captured.

Chief of staff – the most senior officer of an armed force.

Hitler attends a Nazi rally at Nuremberg in 1929.

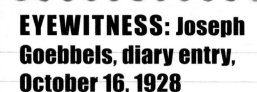

EYEWITNESS: Joseph Goebbels, diary entry, October 16, 1928

"National Socialism is a religion. All we lack is a genius capable of uprooting outmoded religious practices and putting new ones in their place. One day soon National Socialism will be the religion of all Germans. I believe I serve the Lord best if I do his will, and liberate my oppressed people from slavery."

SEPTEMBER 18, 1931, Berlin

Hitler's favorite niece Geli Raubal shoots herself with the Führer's gun after he forbids her to move to Vienna. Hitler slumps into depression.

JUNE 1932, Germany

Chancellor Brüning, feeling confident enough to take a stand against the Nazis, orders the disbandment of the SA and SS under a decree that prohibits uniformed political organizations. By the time the decree comes into effect, the SS has grown to 30,000 members, or approximately 10 percent of the SA's strength.

NOVEMBER 6, 1932, Berlin

In the last of the year's national elections, the Nazi Party loses two million votes and is reduced to 196 seats. The communists gain 750,000 votes and now have 100 seats in the Reichstag.

DECEMBER 1932, Germany

The end of the year sees the political situation degenerate almost into a state of civil war. The socialists and Communist Party field armed militia to battle the right-wing street fighters.

A Nuremberg Rally in the early 1930s shows the power of the Nazis at the time.

Decree – an order that has the same force as a law.

EYEWITNESS: D. Sefton Delmar, Reichstag Fire, Berlin

"'God grant,' Hitler said, 'that this is the work of the Communists. You are witnessing the beginning of a great new epoch in German history. This fire is the beginning. You see this flaming building,' he said, sweeping his hand dramatically around him. 'If this Communist spirit got hold of Europe for but two months it would be all aflame like this building.'"

Under Heinrich Himmler, the SS became a ruthless organization.

JANUARY, Germany

Ex-Chancellor Franz von Papen and Hitler agree to a coalition, with Hitler as its head. The Third Reich is born.

FEBRUARY 27, Germany

The Reichstag building burns down. Blaming the fire on communists, Hitler uses the event as an excuse to expand his powers.

MARCH 22, Germany

An Enabling Law gives Hitler special powers for four years. The law provides the foundations for a dictatorship.

APRIL 1, Germany

Boycott of Jewish shops begins.

MAY 6, Germany

Goebbels organizes the mass burning of "un-German" books.

OCTOBER, Germany

Hitler takes Germany out of the League of Nations.

NOVEMBER 12, Germany

A referendum gives 95 percent approval rating to Nazi policy.

Hitler, now chancellor of Germany, with President Paul von Hindenburg in 1933.

Coalition – a government in which power is shared between parties.

FEBRUARY 3, 1934, Germany
Ernst Röhm begins a campaign to try to strengthen his hold over the veterans of the SA.
.

JUNE 1, Germany
The pocket battleship *Admiral Graf Spee* is launched.

JUNE 14, Italy
German diplomats arrange a meeting between Hitler and Italian dictator Mussolini in Venice.

JUNE 26, Germany
Heinrich Himmler warns senior SS officers of an approaching revolt by the SA.

JUNE 30, Germany
Hitler orders the arrest and murder of SA leaders in a purge known as the Night of the Long Knives; the victims include Röhm, who is shot on July 2. The SA no longer represent a threat to the Nazi leaders.

JULY 14, Germany
A law is issued legitimizing all the killings of the Night of the Long Knives. The SS is now formally separated from the SA.

A Brownshirt stands outside a store as a boycott of Jewish businesses begins.

JULY 25, Austria
Hitler supports an attempt by the Nazis of Vienna to seize power. Mussolini mobilizes his troops to stop any German surge into Austria, halting Nazi plans to absorb Austria.

AUGUST 2, Neudeck
Field Marshal Paul von Hindenburg dies. Hitler combines the role of chancellor with that of president, making him leader of Germany and commander of the armed forces.

TURNING POINTS: Night of the Long Knives

In 1934 the tensions between Hitler and the leadership of the SA peaked. Ernst Röhm wanted the SA to replace the army. Hitler did not want to alienate the army, and, persuaded by senior Nazis including Himmler, Göring and Goebbels, decided to get rid of the SA threat. The result was the Night of the Long Knives. On June 30, 1934, the senior leadership of the SA, including Röhm, was murdered. The army was delighted that the SA was no longer a threat. Just over a month later, however, the army had a new leader. After the death of the president, Paul von Hindenburg, on August 2, Hitler outmaneuvered the army by taking control as commander in chief.

Purge – an operation to get rid of people who are seen as undesirable.

EYEWITNESS: William L. Shirer, reporter, Nuremberg Rally, 1934

"This morning's opening meeting had something of the mysticism and religious fervor of an Easter or Christmas Mass in a great Gothic cathedral. The hall was a sea of brightly colored flags. The band stopped playing. There was a hush over the thirty thousand people in the hall. Then the band struck up. Hitler appeared in the back of the auditorium and followed by his aides he slowly strode down the long aisle while thirty thousand hands were raised in salute."

JANUARY 13, The Saar
The inhabitants of the Saar region on the French border overwhelmingly vote to return to the Reich in a plebiscite.

FEBRUARY 26, Germany
Hitler announces the official formation of the new Luftwaffe (German Air Force).

MARCH 1, The Saar
The German Army, accompanied by armed SS units, marches into Saarbrücken.

MARCH 16, Germany
Hitler overturns the Treaty of Versailles. He reintroduces military conscription.

NOVEMBER, Germany
National Law of Citizenship becomes law. It defines who is a Jew or someone of mixed race. Applicants for public posts must be Aryans. Marriage between Aryans and Jews or those of mixed race is forbidden.

1936

MARCH, Germany
The Locarno Treaty is renounced. This was a nonaggression treaty signed between Germany, France, and Belgium.

MARCH 7, The Rhineland
Hitler orders his army to march into the demilitarized Rhineland.

MAY 8, Dachau
Reichsführer-SS Himmler takes a group of Nazi Party officials around a new concentration camp.

German troops march into the Saar in March following the plebiscite.

Plebiscite – a vote in which a population accepts or rejects a proposal.

A propaganda image shows well-fed inmates in a concentration camp.

JULY 17, Spain
The Spanish Civil War starts.

JULY 11, Germany
Hitler recognizes the sovereignty of Austria. In return, the Austrian chancellor Schuschnigg acknowledges that Austria is a "German state."

JULY 31, Spain
German volunteers travel to Spain to help General Franco.

AUGUST, Berlin
The Olympic Games open.

OCTOBER, Germany
Göring starts the Four-Year Plan with the aim of making Germany industrially independent.

NOVEMBER, Spain
German involvement in the Spanish Civil War becomes primarily a Luftwaffe affair.

NOVEMBER 1, Italy
Mussolini announces a military pact between Italy and Germany.

TURNING POINTS:
The Luftwaffe

In April 1935, the aerial warfare branch of the German Army, the Luftwaffe, formally came into existence under the leadership of Hermann Göring. A fighter squadron was established and the first Luftwaffe fighter school was set up. It completed the formation of the Luftwaffe and the Nationalsozialistische Flieger Korps. Observers were astonished that Hitler, with few resources, had put together a technically accomplished flying force. Its reputation would be cemented by its role in the Spanish Civil War, particularly the bombing of Guernica in 1937.

NOVEMBER 25, Germany
Germany signs a pact with Japan.

DECEMBER 8, Germany
The battlecruiser *Gneisenau* is launched.

Military musicians perform at the Munich Olympic Games in 1936.

Pact – a formal agreement between nations.

TURNING POINTS:
Deutschland Incident

In May 1937, during the Spanish Civil War, Soviet pilots bombed the German battleship *Deutschland*, at anchor in Ibiza harbor. The bombing caused outrage in Nazi Germany, which retaliated by bombing the Spanish city of Almería. The Soviets had, in fact, bombed the German ship by mistake. They had thought they were bombing the *Canarias*, the flagship of the Nationalist leader, General Franco. The *Deutschland* sailed to the Mediterranean island of Gibraltar, where British medical personnel took care of the casualties. The death toll was 31, with a further 74 wounded.

The Duke and Duchess of Windsor arrive in Berlin to visit Hitler in October.

FEBRUARY 6, Germany
The heavy cruiser *Admiral Hipper* is launched. The ship is part of Germany's Plan-Z. The Nazis are trying to build a navy to compete with the British Royal Navy.

APRIL 26, Spain
The bombers of the Condor Legion, from the Luftwaffe, destroy the town of Guernica in the heart of the Basque region on a busy market day. The bombing shocks the world.

JUNE, Germany
Reinhard Heydrich, the head of both the Sicherheitdienst (SD) and the Gestapo, issues secret orders that mean "protective custody" (ie concentration camp) for those jailed for "racial offenses" after release. This means Jews can now be sent to concentration camps for having relationships with Aryans.

AUGUST, Germany
The Minister of Economics, Hjalmar Schacht, resigns. Once a firm follower of Hitler, he has become disillusioned with the Nazis and with the struggle against inflation.

Throughout the 1930s, Hitler built up the German navy.

Retaliated – struck back in reaction to an act of violence.

SEPTEMBER 24, Germany

Mussolini boards a train in Rome bound for Germany and a meeting with Hitler. His nine-coach armored train takes him on an historic journey that will cement the bond between Italy and Germany.

SEPTEMBER 25, Austria

Mussolini's train enters Austria. The Austrian Chancellor, Dr Kurt von Schuschnigg, is worried about an assassination attempt on the Italian dictator but the train passes safely through Austria to the German border.

Hitler and Mussolini drive through Berlin during Mussolini's state visit.

SEPTEMBER 25, Germany

Mussolini arrives in Munich to begin his state visit. Hitler and the other senior Nazis welcome the Italian dictator, who is visibly impressed by the military strength Hitler has on display.

EYEWITNESS: Noel Monks, reporter, Spain, April 26, 1937

"We were still a good 10 miles (16 km) away when I saw the reflection of Guernica's flames in the sky. As we drew nearer, I saw a priest in one group. 'What happened, Father?' I asked. His face was blackened, his clothes in tatters. He couldn't talk. He just pointed to the flames, still about 4 (6 km) miles away, then whispered: 'Aviones, bombas; mucho, mucho.'"

SEPTEMBER 29, Berlin

After a farewell lunch at the Reich Chancellery, Mussolini and Hitler shake hands at Lehrter Station and Mussolini boards his train home. The last few days have made the strength of the Rome-Berlin axis obvious to the whole world.

OCTOBER 22, Berlin

Nazi leaders meet England's Duke and Duchess of Windsor as they arrive in Berlin.

NOVEMBER 1, Germany

The Enabling Law is renewed. This ensures that Germany remains a National Socialist dictatorship. Confiscation of Jewish businesses without legal justification continues.

NOVEMBER 1, Germany

Hellmuth Volkmann is appointed commander of the Condor Legion, a position he will hold for the next year. The legion is flying missions on behalf of Franco's Nationalists in the Spanish Civil War.

Axis – an alliance between countries to promote their shared interests.

TURNING POINTS: The Munich Agreement

Hitler, having absorbed Austria in March 1938, turned his attention to Czechoslovakia. Three million people in the Sudeten area were of German origin. Without consulting the Czechs, the French and British agreed with Hitler that areas with more than 50 percent German populations would be returned to Germany. When Hitler then demanded all of Sudetenland, war loomed. British Prime Minster Chamberlain flew to Munich where Hitler, Mussolini and the French premier Edouard Daladier met on September 29. They agreed that Germany would occupy Sudetenland. Hitler promised this would be his last demand for territory—but he had outmaneuvered the Allied leaders.

Nazi troops march in Vienna following Austria's union with Germany.

FEBRUARY, Germany

Hitler becomes Minister of War and Commander-in-Chief of the armed forces. He now has the complete loyalty of the army. Ribbentrop is appointed Foreign Minister. Austrian Chancellor Schuschnigg is summoned to Germany and given an ultimatum to allow the Nazis a free hand in Austria.

MARCH 12, Austria

The Anschluss ("Union") with Austria means that all laws of Germany are now the laws of Austria. Austria has ceased to be a sovereign country as Germany invades. The enthusiastic welcome from Austrians persuades Hitler to annex Austria fully on March 13.

APRIL 10, Austria

A controlled vote (plebiscite) gives a 99.7 percent vote of approval for the Nazis' actions in Austria.

JUNE, Munich

Nazis destroy a synagogue. A new decree demands registration of all Jewish businesses.

JULY, Germany

Prime Minister Chamberlain of Great Britain visits Hitler at Berchtesgaden to discuss Hitler's demands for territory from Czechoslovakia.

AUGUST, Germany

General Ludwig Beck, Chief of the General Staff, tries to warn the British of Hitler's plans. He also writes to the commander of the German army, Walther von Brauchitsch, warning of the dangers of war. Beck is forced to resign.

Ultimatum – a demand which, if it is not met, will lead to war.

AUGUST, Nuremberg

A new decree is issued requiring all Jews to carry the first name of either "Israel" or "Sarah" from 1939.

SEPTEMBER, Munich

British Prime Minister Chamberlain meets with Hitler, Daladier, and Mussolini in Munich. They agree that the Sudetenland area of Czechoslovakia should go to Germany. Both Britain and France are eager to avoid making a stand that could lead to war.

Agreement in Munich failed to halt Hitler's demands for more territory.

OCTOBER 1, Sudetenland

Germany occupies the Sudetenland in accordance with the Munich Agreement.

NOVEMBER 9, Germany

Heydrich organizes Kristallnacht ("Crystal Night"). In the pogrom, more than 20,000 Jews are imprisoned, and 74 killed. Synagogues and Jewish businesses are attacked. The name Kristallnacht comes from the fragments of glass from smashed windows. President Roosevelt recalls the U.S. ambassador from Germany.

DECEMBER, Germany

Compulsory Aryanization of all Jewish shops and firms. Jews no longer play any part in the German economy.

German troops are welcomed as they march into the Sudetenland.

EYEWITNESS: Firefighter, Laupheim, Kristallnacht,

"I was not allowed to go into the firehouse to take the engines out. One of my friends whispered to me, 'Be quiet – the Synagogue is burning; I was beaten up when I wanted to put out the fire.' Eventually we were allowed to take the fire engines out, but only very slowly. We were ordered not to use any water till the whole synagogue was burned down."

Pogrom – the organized, often official, persecution of a minority, such as Jews.

FEBRUARY 14, Germany

The battleship *Bismarck* is launched.

MARCH, Czechoslovakia

Germany occupies Bohemia and Moravia as "protectorates," finally destroying Czechoslovakia. Memel is annexed from Lithuania. The Germans now claim the Free City of Danzig in Poland and the "Polish Corridor," a narrow strip of land that joins East Prussia to the rest of Germany.

APRIL, Germany

Jewish valuables are confiscated and a new law makes all Jews live together in "Jewish homes."

APRIL 2, Spain

The Spanish Civil War officially ends.

MAY 19, Spain

A victory parade is held in Madrid to celebrate the triumph of General Franco's Nationalists in the Civil War.

TURNING POINTS: Condor Legion

The Condor Legion was a bomber unit of volunteers from the Luftwaffe and the Wehrmacht. They fought with the Nationalists in the Spanish Civil War, from July 1936 to March 1939. The Condor Legion devised the use of terror bombing, which was also used in World War II. The Condor Legion was responsible for the bombing of the Spanish city of Guernica, which shocked the world in April 1937.

MAY 30, Hamburg

The Condor Legion—the Luftwaffe that flew in the Spanish Civil War—lands at Hamburg, where it is greeted by Hermann Göring.

JUNE 6, Germany

The Condor Legion makes its last public appearance. At a special military parade, Hitler reviews more than 14,000 troops from the Legion.

JULY, Germany

Hitler's Foreign Minister Ribbentrop starts trade talks with the Soviet Union.

AUGUST 23, Germany

Ribbentrop and his Soviet counterpart, Molotov, sign the Russo-German Non-Aggression Treaty. This states that neither party would attack the other and spheres of influence were agreed in the Baltic States and Poland.

German troops arrive in Bohemia in March after it is made a protectorate.

Annex – to incorporate territory into an existing country.

AUGUST 25, Germany

Hitler orders an attack against Poland, to take place that afternoon. Two hours later, the German Army in the East leaves to begin the invasion. Hitler then changes his mind when he receives a letter from the British government reaffirming its intention to help Poland if Germany invades. Hitler stops the invasion.

AUGUST 25, Great Britain

In the face of growing German aggression, an Anglo–Polish treaty of mutual assistance is signed; Britain will help Poland if it is attacked.

Hitler intended to seize the Free City of Danzig for Germany.

AUGUST 28, Berlin

At 22.00 hours at the Chancellery, Sir Neville Henderson, the British ambassador, meets Hitler to deliver another letter from the British government confirming Britain's intention to stand by Poland.

AUGUST 30, Poland

Poland orders the mobilization of its armed forces. Hitler gives the order to invade Poland at 04.45 hours. To legitimize the invasion he orders the Gleiwitz plan to be put into action. This is an attack by the SS on the radio station in the German border town of Gleiwitz, carefully staged to make it look like the work of Polish troops. Hitler now has his justification for invading Poland.

Stalin's foreign secretary, Molotov (right), negotiated a treaty with Germany.

EYEWITNESS: Luise Solmitz, housewife, Hamburg, August 1939

"Who is going to help tortured humanity away from war to peace? Easy to answer: nothing and no one. A butchery is beginning such as the world has not yet experienced. A world full of blood and atrocity. And so we enter a time that has been dreaded and feared, a time in comparison to which the 30 Years' War was a Sunday School outing... Now that Europe's wounds have been healed after 21 years, the West will be annihilated."

Mobilization – an order to a country's armed forces to make ready for war.

Swastikas fly in Danzig after the end of the campaign in Poland.

EYEWITNESS: Melitha Maschmann, Hitler Youth press officer, November 1939

"I told myself that if the Poles were using every means not to lose that disputed province which the German nation required as 'Lebensraum' (living space), they remained our enemies... A group which believes itself chosen to lead, as we did, has no inhibitions about taking territory from 'inferior elements.'"

SEPTEMBER 1, Poland

The incident at Gleiwitz is reported in the German press. Hitler tells his armed forces he can see no way to halt "persecution" of Germans in Poland except through war.

SEPTEMBER 3, North Sea

German ships start laying mines, concentrating on the defence of the German Bight.

SEPTEMBER 3, Europe

Great Britain and France declare war on Germany. The Soviet Union invades Poland.

SEPTEMBER 3, Germany

Jews are forbidden to be outside after 9.00 p.m. All radios belonging to Jews are confiscated.

SEPTEMBER 17, Atlantic Ocean

The British aircraft carrier HMS *Courageous* is sunk by the German submarine *U-29*.

OCTOBER, Poland

German armies advance rapidly through Poland. Meanwhile the Germans plan to begin Operation Yellow, the invasion of France through the Low Countries.

German motorized infantry advance into Poland during the Blitzkrieg.

OCTOBER 4, Atlantic Ocean

German Naval Command intensifies the war against Allied merchant shipping.

OCTOBER 13, Scapa Flow

U-47 penetrates the Royal Navy defenses at Scapa Flow in a daring night raid that sinks the battleship HMS *Royal Oak*.

NOVEMBER 9, France

There is little military action on the Western Front. This period is known as the "Sitzkrieg" or sitting war.

NOVEMBER 30, Finland

Russia attacks Finland, but the invasion is carried out so inefficiently it suggests that the Red Army is not a high-quality fighting force.

DECEMBER, Norway

Admiral Raeder, commander of the German Navy, urges Hitler to take Norway so that Britain does not block the sea route used to transport Swedish iron-ore to Germany.

The *Admiral Graf Spee* burns after being scuttled in Montevideo harbor.

DECEMBER 17, Atlantic Ocean

The Battle of the River Plate. After sinking several British merchant ships in the Atlantic, the German heavy cruiser *Admiral Graf Spee* flees from British cruisers to Montevideo harbor in Uruguay for repairs. British vessels begin to gather in anticipation of a naval clash. Instead, the captain of the *Admiral Graf Spee* orders his crew to scuttle their ship. Three days later, he shoots himself.

TURNING POINTS: Scapa Flow

Scapa Flow was a Royal Navy anchorage in sheltered waters in the Orkney Islands off the northeast coast of Scotland. On the night of October 13/14, 1939, the German submarine *U-47*, commanded by Günther Prien, penetrated the defenses of the base. Commanding his first submarine, Prien made a daring attack on the Royal Navy warships. First, he attacked the battleship HMS *Royal Oak*, which sank with the loss of its crew of 883. He then hit and damaged the aircraft carrier HMS *Pegasus*, which he mistook for the *Repulse*. Hitler rewarded Prien with the Knight's Cross of the Iron Cross, making him only the second naval officer to be decorated with this distinction. The spectacular blow against the Royal Navy was a great boost to German morale.

The German ship *Altmark* was used to hold British prisoners in Norway.

FEBRUARY 15, Atlantic Ocean

Hitler gives order for an unlimited U-boat war to stop supplies getting through to Britain from the United States. Any ship that might be under British control can now be torpedoed.

MARCH 11, Finland

Finland signs a peace treaty with the Soviet Union, ceding territory around the Baltic Sea.

MARCH 11, Scandinavia

Hitler orders an attack on Norway and Denmark.

APRIL 9, Norway

The invasion of Denmark and Norway begins. In Denmark, there is almost no resistance. Fighting is heavier in Norway but Germany will still take the country after a campaign lasting 62 days.

APRIL 14, Norway

Anglo-French troops land at Narvik and Trondheim, but achieve little.

MAY 10, Norway

Allied troops leave. The Germans now control most of Norway.

MAY 10, Belgium

Hitler launches Operation Yellow, a push through the Ardennes.

MAY 11, Belgium

German paratroopers take the fortress at Eben Emael.

MAY 15, Holland

The Dutch Army surrenders.

MAY 17, Belgium

Brussels, the capital city, falls.

MAY 20, France

German troops reach the Channel coast, cutting French and British forces off from each other.

MAY 27, Dunkirk

The British start evacuating troops from the beaches to England.

German troops advance in Norway following an artillery barrage.

Cede – to give up or surrender territory.

General Irwin Rommel (center) led the German Panzers to the English Channel.

MAY 27, Belgium

King Leopold of Belgium surrenders.

JUNE 3, Germany

The Dunkirk evacuation ends after rescuing more than 300,000 soldiers.

JUNE 5, France

The German Army resumes its offensive, moving south and west into France to encircle a large part of the remaining French army.

EYEWITNESS: Walter Mauth, schoolboy, Berlin

"Everywhere the war lasted three or four weeks and everything went like clockwork. German soldiers were obviously unstoppable. We were all, to be honest, enthusiastic, even those who had previously had a different attitude toward the entire regime. All of a sudden considering everything worked so well and nobody had been able to stop us, we were suddenly all nationalists."

JUNE 10, France

Italy declares war on Great Britain and France. It moves troops into southern France.

JUNE 14, France

German troops enter Paris.

TURNING POINTS: Missed Chance at Dunkirk

By May 20, 1940, the German take-over of France was well underway. The German Army had reached the English Channel and succeeded in splitting the Allied forces in two. The German commander-in-chief, von Brauchitsch, wanted to finish the job by rounding up the Anglo-French and Belgian troops. Instead, General von Rundstedt, supported by Hitler, decided to stop his troops and regroup. Hitler wanted Göring's Luftwaffe to have a chance to distinguish itself by destroying the Allied forces trapped into the Dunkirk Pocket, but bombing failed to destroy the troops. Instead, thousands of British volunteers sailing small boats performed a major evacuation of troops from Dunkirk. More than 300,000 soldiers were rescued, enabling the British to keep fighting.

Evacuation – a large-scale operation to remove people from danger to safety.

JUNE 21, France

The French surrender is signed. France is divided into the occupied north and "Vichy," governed by the French as a German puppet state.

JUNE 27, Atlantic Ocean

Great Britain announces a total blockade of the Continent.

JULY 19, Berlin

A victory parade is held to celebrate the stunning victory in the West.

AUGUST, Soviet Union

Hitler secretly orders his staff to prepare a plan to invade the Soviet Union (codenamed "Otto"), while at the same time also making plans to invade Great Britain.

AUGUST 8, Great Britain

Aldertag or Eagle Day, the codename for the first day of the air offensive against Great Britain, is launched (in Britain, this is known as the Battle of Britain).

The World War I hero Marshal Pétain became leader of Vichy France.

AUGUST 20, Gibraltar

The German High Command plans to capture Gibraltar in Operation "Felix."

AUGUST 27, Great Britain

The Germans abandon plans for a large-scale invasion in favor of a series of smaller landings along the English coast.

AUGUST 30, Great Britain

With the failure of the Luftwaffe to defeat the Royal Air Force (RAF), the invasion is indefinitely postponed.

TURNING POINTS: The Fall of Greece

One of the least expected campaigns of the war was the Italian invasion of Greece. Although Adolf Hitler had expressed his wish to keep the Balkans out of the war, Mussolini could not resist the temptation to fulfil his ambition to create a "New Roman Empire." Mussolini realized he did not have the means to wage war on a grand scale, so he selected Greece as a potentially easy target. Some 70,000 Italian troops invaded on October 28. Just two weeks later, the Italian invasion force was in full retreat in the face of Greek resistance supported by the British Royal Air Force. In April 1941, the Germans invaded in support of their allies. They conquered the whole of Greece in only three weeks.

Puppet state – a government that obeys the government of another country.

EYEWITNESS: Albert Speer, on Hitler's visit to Paris

"By nine o'clock in the morning the sightseeing tour was over. 'It was the dream of my life to be permitted to see Paris. I cannot say how happy I am to have that dream fulfilled today.' For a moment I felt something like pity for him: three hours in Paris, the one and only time he was to see it, made him happy when he stood at the height of his triumphs."

Italian artillery pounds Greek positions during Mussolini's ill-fated invasion.

SEPTEMBER 27, Japan

Japan joins the Axis of Germany and Italy. The three pledge to fight any state that declares war on any one of them.

OCTOBER 7, Romania

Germany invades Romania, seizing the vital oilfields at Ploesti.

OCTOBER 28, Balkans

Despite Hitler's wish that there is no conflict in the southern Balkans, Italian forces cross the Greek frontier to start one of the most surprising campaigns of World War II.

Mussolini has gone against the express wishes of Hitler, who eventually has to go to his ally's aid to avoid an Italian defeat.

NOVEMBER, Germany

Hungary, Romania, and Slovakia sign treaties with Germany.

DECEMBER 18, Soviet Union

Hitler issues Directive No.21, calling for Operation Barbarossa to be launched around May 15, 1941. The invasion of the Soviet Union will be led by three million German troops.

German troops practice with landing craft for the invasion of Great Britain.

Directive – an order or instruction issued by a central authority.

KEY PEOPLE: Rudolf Hess

Rudolf Hess was an early devotee of Adolf Hitler. Seduced by Hitler's rhetoric, he joined the Nazis in 1920. He marched in the 1923 Putsch and was imprisoned with Hitler. While in jail, he worked as Hitler's secretary; Hitler dictated his book, *Mein Kampf*, to Hess. When Hitler came to power, Hess became deputy leader, but by 1939 his power had waned. He felt estranged from Hitler and overtaken by Göring and Himmler. To try to recover his position with Hitler, Hess secretly flew alone to Britain in May 1941 to try to achieve a peace agreement. The plan failed and Hess was imprisoned. After the Nuremberg Trials, he remained in jail until he committed suicide in 1987.

JANUARY, North Africa

The Afrika Korps is formed for the Libya Campaign. Italian troops are in bad shape and unable to defend Mussolini's remaining North Africa possessions after a series of heavy defeats at the hands of the British. Hitler is forced to come to the help of his ally.

FEBRUARY, Bulgaria

Hitler occupies Bulgaria from his bases in Romania to pre-empt a suspected Soviet move.

MARCH 2, Balkans

Hitler persuades Yugoslavia to become a member of the Axis treaty.

MARCH 3, Great Britain

The British capture an "Enigma"-type cipher machine from a Nazi E-boat. This will prove a turning point in Britain's war against the Nazis.

APRIL 6, Balkans

Germany invades and occupies Yugoslavia and Greece. Hungarian troops also attack Yugoslavia and its government surrenders. German troops occupy Greece, brushing aside the small British army there.

APRIL 6, Libya

With three reinforced Italian Army corps and the German 15th Panzer Division, Rommel moves through Libya toward Egypt. At Tobruk, the 1st Australian Division holds him off and is left in a state of siege.

APRIL 27, Greece

German troops occupy Athens.

German panzers enter the Greek port of Thessalonika in April.

Siege – a military operation in which a town or position is cut off.

The advance guard of the Leibstandarte-SS Adolf Hitler crosses the gulf of Corinth in requisitioned Greek fishing boats. Commonwealth troops are evacuated to the island of Crete.

MAY, Germany

Heydrich prepares the SS for its role in the forthcoming war in the Soviet Union. He instructs the leaders of the *Einsatzgruppen* (Special Task Force) on their mission to murder all Jews, "Asiatics," Communist officials, intellectuals, professionals, and Gypsies.

German motorized troops at the start of Operation Barbarossa in June.

MAY 10, Great Britain

Rudolf Hess flies to Great Britain, seeking an audience with King George VI. He wants the king to dismiss the Prime Minister, Winston Churchill, and then make peace with Germany. The British immediately imprison Hess.

MAY 20, Balkans

German paratroopers land on Crete and take the island despite incurring heavy casualties.

MAY 24, Atlantic Ocean

The British battlecruiser HMS *Hood* is sunk by the *Bismarck*; three days later the *Bismarck* is sunk during a battle with Royal Navy ships.

A panzer advances toward Egypt in the Afrika Korps' first offensive.

EYEWITNESS: Erich Hoepner, IV Panzer Corps

"The war against Russia is a fundamental part of the German people's struggle for existence. It is the old struggle of the Germans against the Slavs, the defense of European culture against the Muscovite, Asiatic deluge, the defense against Jewish Bolshevism. This struggle must aim to smash Russia into rubble, and as a consequence it must be carried out with unprecedented harshness."

Requisition – to seize private property for official use.

A Red Army soldier surrenders to the Germans during Operation Barbarossa.

JULY, Soviet Union

Göring orders Heydrich to clear the occupied lands in the Soviet Union of Jews. The SS *Einsatzgruppen* follow the German armies and begin executing Jews and other people they call "sub-humans."

AUGUST, Soviet Union

The German advance in the East continues. Estonia is occupied and incorporated into a new territory called Ostland. British and Soviet troops move into Iran to prevent a German linkup in the Middle East.

JUNE 22, Soviet Union

Operation Barbarossa, the German invasion of the Soviet Union by three million German, Romanian, Finnish, Hungarian, and Slovak troops, begins. The Russians are taken completely by surprise, despite numerous warnings. All Red Army political commissars are to be killed on capture. General orders are issued to all the German troops to be ruthless against the "Bolshevik" Russians.

SEPTEMBER 1, Germany

Wearing a yellow star becomes compulsory for Jews living in Germany. The general deportation of German Jews to concentration camps begins.

SEPTEMBER 19, Ukraine

Having already occupied most of the Ukraine, German troops take the capital, Kiev. The siege of Leningrad in the Soviet Union begins.

TURNING POINTS: Operation Barbarossa

Operation Barbarossa was the codename of the German invasion of the Soviet Union, which began on June 22, 1941. The invasion directly contradicted the nonaggression pact between the Soviets and the Germans. Stalin refused to believe intelligence reports about an imminent German attack. The Russian command was taken by surprise, and in the first weeks of the operation the Germans scored stunning victories against an unprepared and ill-trained Red Army. German troops took Ukraine and its capital Kiev before moving toward Moscow in Operation Typhoon. On October 1, Hitler described the extent of his victory: 2.5 million prisoners taken, 22,000 guns captured, 18,000 tanks destroyed, and 145,000 Russian aircraft eliminated.

Commissars – Soviet personnel who educated troops in Communist ideology.

German soldiers trudge through the snow on the retreat from Moscow.

OCTOBER 1, Soviet Union

The German Army begins Operation Typhoon, the offensive against Moscow. Hitler boasts about the approaching glorious victory to the German public, but despite heavy losses, the Red Army still exists as a fighting force.

NOVEMBER 27, Moscow

The German drive toward Moscow starts to falter. The German troops are hungry and sick with fatigue, and are slowed down by heavy rains and severe frosts. The winter conditions halt them 20 miles (32 km) from Moscow.

DECEMBER 5, Soviet Union

To the surprise of the German General Staff and the confusion of frontline troops around Moscow, Russian counterattacks come through the snow using reserves from Siberia who are better equipped for winter than the Germans.

DECEMBER 7, Pearl Harbor

The Japanese attack Pearl Harbor and part of the U.S. Pacific Fleet is destroyed.

DECEMBER 11, Germany and Italy

Germany and Italy declare war on the United States. This is an ill-advised gesture of solidarity with Japan that will prove to have significant consequences for Germany in the long term.

The *Bismarck*, pride of the German fleet, was sunk in May 1942.

EYEWITNESS: Bishop of Munster, sermon against euthanasia, August 1941

"We are not dealing with machines, horses, and cows whose only function is to serve mankind, to produce goods for man... No, we are dealing with human beings, our fellow human beings, our brothers and sisters. Have they forfeited the right to life? Have you, have I the right to live only so long as we are productive?"

Euthanasia – a policy of deliberately killing "unproductive" individuals.

Officers of the Afrika Korps watch a bombardment of Tobruk.

JANUARY 21, Libya

Rommel has been forced to retreat and the British Eighth Army has moved back into Libya. Rommel awaits reinforcements and then attacks the British. Benghazi falls by the 29th.

FEBRUARY 4, Libya

Rommel nears Tobruk but his lines of communication are stretched.

FEBRUARY 11, English Channel

The Kriegsmarine achieve a great propaganda victory as three ships sail through the English Channel from Brest, France, to Germany and Norway in the so-called "Channel dash."

JANUARY 1, Washington D.C.

America, Britain, the Soviet Union, and the other Allied nations agree that none of them will make separate peace treaties with Germany.

JANUARY 20, Berlin

Nazi Party and government officials meet at a conference in Wannsee, a Berlin suburb, to discuss the Jewish "problem." They agree to implement "the Final Solution." This will involve rounding up some 11 million European Jews to be deported to labor camps in the East. Within a few weeks, the first gas chambers for mass killings are built in concentration camps in Poland.

Reinhard Heydrich's funeral in Berlin, after his assassination in June 1942.

EYEWITNESS: Joachim Stempel, 14th Panzer Division, Stalingrad

"There were snipers firing from everywhere, from any hole, from any corner, from any chimney of a burned-down house, from any pile of earth... A lot of women in uniform proved to be excellent snipers and made our life there a living hell. You had to make your way to the front, ducking, crouching, kneeling and shots rang out from all sides... and all around you was the noise of artillery salvoes hitting what was left of the buildings..."

Propaganda – material intended to influence public opinion.

TURNING POINTS: The Wansee Conference

Hosted by Reinhard Heydrich, the Wannsee Conference gathered Nazi Party and government officials in the SS headquarters in the Wannsee suburb of Berlin on January 20, 1942. The meeting lasted only a few hours but had devastating consequences. The meeting discussed ways to get rid of millions of Jews in German-occupied territory, including sterilization and mass deportation. Instead, the "Final Solution" was proposed. Jews were to be moved east to work in labor gangs. Hard work and little food would result in significant loss of life. To accelerate the process, poison gas chambers were built in Poland. Responsibility for carrying out the decisions made at Wannsee was given to Heinrich Himmler, the head of the SS.

MAY 8, Crimea

The German Army, under Manstein, enters Crimea and besieges Sevastopol, which falls in July. Hitler then sends Manstein north to Leningrad to tackle the siege, which has been going on since September 1941.

MAY 26, Libya

Rommel's Afrika Korps outflanks the British and attacks toward Tobruk. He succeeds in driving the British out of Libya.

MAY 26, Germany

British air raids on German cities intensify.

British infantry capture one of Rommel's panzers near El Alamein.

MAY 27, Czechoslovakia

A plan devised in London for the assassination of Reinhard Heydrich is carried out by British-trained Czech nationalists. After the assassination attempt, Himmler orders the arrest of 10,000 hostages from amongst the Czech intelligentsia. One hundred of the most important are shot that same night.

JUNE 4, Czechoslovakia

Heydrich dies from blood poisoning in Prague.

JUNE 10, Czechoslovakia

Karl Frank, Heydrich's deputy, orders reprisals for the assassination. Hitler orders the destruction of the village of Lidice, which Frank claims has harbored the assassins. At 2.00 a.m. on June 10, SS troops round up all the villagers. Some 197 men are herded onto a farm and killed; all the women and children are loaded onto trucks and sent to concentration camps. The village is bulldozed. The Nazis announce that Lidice has ceased to exist.

Outflank – to pass around the side of an enemy force.

Allied air raids struck many German cities, including Cologne.

JUNE 21, Libya

The British retreat into Egypt, having lost Tobruk after a fierce battle. Rommel is promoted to field marshal.

JUNE 21, Poland

Mass gassings begin at the Auschwitz concentration camp in Poland.

JULY 4, Crimea

The Germans take Sevastopol.

JULY 13, Ukraine

Hitler moves to his Ukraine headquarters to supervise the summer offensive and the Sixth Army's advance on Stalingrad and the Caucasus. Initial progress is good.

AUGUST 19, France

In a rehearsal for an Allied landing in France, 5,000 Canadian and 1,000 British troops take part in a disastrous raid on Dieppe, France. Some 4,000 men are killed or captured.

SEPTEMBER 1, Caucasus

German troops enter Stalingrad and reach the Elbruz Mountains in the Caucasus.

OCTOBER 14, Schweinfurt

A catastrophic raid by 291 American B-17E "Flying Fortresses" on the ball-bearing factories at Schweinfurt highlights the problems of daylight bombing. Waves of German fighters shoot down 60 bombers and badly damage another 138. The Allies cannot sustain such a heavy loss rate.

TURNING POINTS: Stalingrad

In the summer of 1942 the Germans advanced to the suburbs of Stalingrad but failed to take the city in the face of determined defense. By September, the Germans had reached the city center, where they met the Soviet Sixty-Second Army. By mid-October the Soviets had been driven back almost to the Volga River. Now, however, German supplies started to run low and their tanks were useless in street fighting. On November 19, the Soviets launched a counterattack. By the 23rd, they had encircled the Germans. A relief attempt failed but Hitler ordered the troops to fight on. In early January 1943, Field Marshal Paulus surrendered the German Sixth Army. Axis losses were estimated at 800,000, and Soviet soldiers at 1.1 million.

Commandos – soldiers specially trained to operate in small groups.

EYEWITNESS: Geoffrey Talbot, reporter, El Alamein, November 1, 1942

"With the sand clouds whirling up behind each vehicle, British tanks in large numbers are moving into battle. Shells by the thousand are being pumped into the enemy, and we are at the side of one of these desert tracks watching the armed might of the 8th Army go forward to engage the enemy."

A Luftwaffe airplane is fueled in the failed operation to relieve Stalingrad.

OCTOBER 23, Egypt

The British defeat Rommel at El Alamein after a week of hard fighting. Despite losing four times as many tanks as the Germans, the British still have plenty of tanks available: 800 versus the Germans' 90. Having overstretched his supply lines, Rommel has no choice but to withdraw or see his Afrika Korps destroyed.

OCTOBER 24, Germany

Hitler holds a meeting with Marshal Pétain, the president of Vichy France, which gives rise to secret accords known as Montoir. Pétain agrees to support Germany's defeat of Britain in every way short of military involvement.

NOVEMBER 9, Stalingrad

The Russians at Stalingrad launch a huge counterattack against Germany's Sixth Army. Hitler refuses to consider a withdrawal to the Don River.

DECEMBER 31, Arctic Ocean

Battle of the North Cape. Hitler is furious after the German North Norway Naval Squadron fails to destroy convoy JW51B. He threatens to "throw the surface fleet into the dustbin."

Men of the German Sixth Army take cover near Stalingrad.

Accords – compromises between conflicting views.

Axis troops retreat following the disaster at Stalingrad.

JANUARY 1, Caucasus

A Red Army offensive retakes Voronezh on the River Don. The Soviets might have cut off the Wehrmacht in the Caucasus, but the German retreat is well organized and avoids the closing Soviet net.

JANUARY 30, Berlin

Grand-Admiral Erich Raeder resigns as Supreme Commander-in-Chief of the Kriegsmarine. Karl Dönitz replaces him.

FEBRUARY 2, Stalingrad

Encircled by the Soviet Offensive, Field Marshal Paulus surrenders with his army at Stalingrad, despite the fact that Hitler has deliberately promoted him in order to encourage Paulus to commit suicide. He and his 90,000 survivors become prisoners of the Soviets. Hitler is furious. From now on he will rely on the Waffen-SS rather than the regular army as his elite fighting force. He allows the SS to take in conscripts and to double in size.

FEBRUARY 22, Munich

Hans and Sophie Scholl of the White Rose resistance group are executed for having distributed anti-Nazi leaflets.

MARCH 13, Germany

General von Tresckow, a highly decorated Prussian officer, organizes an attempt to assassinate Hitler. The Smolensk Plot fails when two bombs, disguised as bottles of brandy on Hitler's plane, fail to explode.

MARCH 14, Kharkov

German tanks and infantry enter Kharkov. After two months of bitter fighting, the SS Panzer Corps manages not only to hold the German line but also to encircle and capture part of the Soviet First Guards Army and an army group, but the Germans sustain heavy casualties in the process.

EYEWITNESS: Joseph Goebbels, speech, February 18, 1943

"I ask you:... Are you resolved to follow the Führer through thick and thin to victory, and are you willing to accept the heaviest personal burdens in the fight for victory?... Are you and the German people willing to work, if the Führer orders, 10, 12 and if necessary 14 hours a day and to give everything for victory? I ask you: Do you want total war? If necessary, do you want a war more total and radical than anything that we can even imagine today?"

Conscripts – soldiers who are forced to serve in the military.

KEY PEOPLE: Hermann Göring

A decorated pilot in World War I, Göring (1893–1946) was head of the Luftwaffe and in 1939 was named Hitler's successor. He planned the Luftwaffe's role in the invasions of Poland, Norway, and France. In 1940, Göring's achievements were recognized by Hitler, who gave him the unique rank of Reichsmarschall. This was the peak of Göring's career. More ambitious Nazis, such as Himmler, Bormann, Goebbels, and Speer, soon overtook him and his importance to Hitler and the Nazis was reduced. At the Nuremberg Trial, he was found guilty of war crimes and sentenced to death. He cheated the hangman by taking cyanide in jail on October 15, 1946.

MARCH 16, Atlantic Ocean

The start of the largest convoy battle of World War II sees German U-boats attacking two Allied convoys.

APRIL 19, Warsaw

The Jews of the Warsaw Ghetto rise up against the Germans. Organized by the Jewish Combat Organization, the fighters hold off the Germans for four weeks. Despite their resistance, by mid-May the Ghetto no longer exists. Around 60,000 Jews have been killed, although they have managed to kill some 1,300 Germans.

Jews of the Warsaw Ghetto are lined up prior to being shot.

APRIL 19, Yugoslavia

Led by Marshal Tito, the number of Yugoslav partisans, or guerrilla fighters, is growing rapidly; it will reach nearly 250,000 by the end of the year.

MAY 13, Tunisia

Around 150,000 Afrika Korps and Italian troops surrender to Allied forces at Tunis. Rommel escapes with a few troops.

MAY 23, Atlantic Ocean

As U-boat losses rise dramatically, Karl Dönitz admits defeat in the Battle of the Atlantic. He withdraws his U-boats from the area.

German panzers advance to meet U.S. forces in Tunisia in February.

Ghetto – part of a city occupied by an ethnic group, because of discrimination.

A panzer commander watches from his turret during the Battle of Kursk.

EYEWITNESS: Johann Johannsen, Hamburg, July 1943

"High above us we could hear the drone of the enemy machines. Suddenly the whole city was lit up in a magically bright light. Before and behind our battery heavy chunks of metal were striking. Howling and hissing, fire and iron were falling from the sky. The whole city was lit up in a sea of flames!"

MAY 29, Germany

An RAF bombing raid destroys 90 percent of Barmen-Wupptertal in just one night. Hitler refuses to visit bomb-damaged cities. He even orders his chauffeur to avoid driving past the bombed areas of Berlin.

JULY 5, Kursk

The Battle of Kursk. The Germans fail in a massive assault on the salient, or bulge, in the Soviet line around the city of Kursk. The Battle of Kursk is the largest tank battle in history, involving 6,000 tanks. Although the battle has no decisive outcome, it is a strategic victory for the Soviets. It marks the end of the German attacks in the East and clears the way for the Soviets to launch a westward offensive.

JULY 10, Italy

Anglo-American forces from North Africa, commanded by the British General Bernard Montgomery and the U.S. General George S. Patton, land in southern Sicily.

Allied vehicles go ashore during Operation Husky, the invasion of Sicily.

Strategic – related to the overall aims of a campaign, not to immediate results.

JULY 11, Italy

Mussolini is dismissed as Prime Minister and imprisoned. It looks as though Italy will fall to Allied forces. Against military advice, Hitler rushes the elite SS Leibstandarte Division from Kursk to Italy, while German forces take over the country and disarm Italian troops.

JULY 29, Germany

Goebbels visits bomb-damaged areas of Germany and writes of his shock at the devastation.

SEPTEMBER 12, Italy

A German commando squad led by Otto Skorzeny launches a daring glider raid to rescue Mussolini from the mountaintop hotel where he has been imprisoned. Mussolini is installed as head of a new puppet government in northern Italy.

SEPTEMBER 26, Norway

British midget submarines, known as X-craft, successfully attack and damage the German battleship *Tirpitz* as it lies at anchor in a Norwegian fjord.

The Tiger tank was Germany's most powerful armored vehicle.

NOVEMBER 6, Ukraine

The Soviets recapture Kiev.

DECEMBER 26, Atlantic Ocean

Dönitz orders the *Scharnhorst* to attack a convoy in the Battle of the North Cape. Warned by decoded messages, the British attack the *Scharnhorst*, which sinks with the loss of almost all its crew.

TURNING POINT: Sinking of the *Scharnhorst*

Hitler had been critical of the German naval fleet, but Admiral Karl Dönitz, head of the navy, persuaded him to let the battlecruisers *Scharnhorst* and *Tirpitz* sail to Norway to harass Russian convoys. With the *Tirpitz* damaged, the *Scharnhorst* carried on alone. On December 19, 1943, Admiral Dönitz told Hitler that *Scharnhorst* would soon attack an Allied convoy. A week later, the pride of the Germany Navy lay at the bottom of the Barents Sea, sunk during the Battle of the North Cape. The British had decoded its orders and were lying in wait. The *Scharnhorst* was hit repeatedly before being torpedoed and sunk. The entire crew of 1,968 was lost, except for 36 men. The sinking was an enormous psychological blow to the Germans.

Convoy – a group of merchant ships traveling together for protection.

TURNING POINTS: D-Day Landings

On June 6, 1944, the British and Americans launched Operation Overlord, the invasion of Normandy in France. The invasion began before dawn, with units of the U.S. 82nd and 101st Airborne Divisions making night landings near the town of Sainte-Mere-Eglise, while British commando units captured key bridges and knocked out Nazi communications. In the morning, landing craft landed thousands of Allied assault troops on five beaches, codenamed Utah, Omaha, Gold, Juno, and Sword. Four beaches fell quickly, but German resistance at Omaha was stiff. However, by nightfall, sizeable beachheads had been secured on all five beaches. From this platform, the Allies went on to launch the final campaign to defeat Germany.

JANUARY 14, Leningrad

The siege is lifted. The German blockade and siege has killed around one million Leningraders. Most have died from starvation, exposure, disease, and shelling. The survivors have been kept alive by supplies brought in across a frozen lake on sleds.

The German battleship *Tirpitz* remained holed up in a Norwegian ford.

JANUARY 21, Anzio

To aid the advance north from the foot of Italy, the Allies make an amphibious landing behind German lines at Anzio, south of Rome. They intend to break the Gustav Line, a German defensive line across the Italian peninsula centered on Monte Cassino. The plan is to cut the German Tenth Army's lines of communication and enable the Allies to march on Rome. However, the American commander General Lucas fails to seize his chance to break out of the bridgehead.

JANUARY 30, Anzio

The eventual U.S. attempt to breakout from the Anzio bridgehead finds the Germans have now organized solid defenses.

FEBRUARY 26, Baltic

The German Army loses Porkhov in the face of the Red Army offensive. Nikopol, with its manganese-ore mines, is abandoned and Krivoi Rog is lost by the end of the month.

MARCH 19, Hungary

As Soviet forces reach the Carpathians, Hitler orders the occupation of Hungary.

Amphibious – describes an operation that lands troops ashore from the sea.

The Germans developed the V-1 rocket to strike at long-distance targets.

JUNE, Germany

The Abwehr, the German military intelligence organization, is closed. Its head, Admiral Canaris, is dismissed on suspicion of being part of the anti-Hitler resistance. Although nothing is proved, Canaris is indeed a member of the organization.

JUNE 6, Normandy

Operation "Overlord", the D-Day Anglo-American landings, begins. In the morning, assault troops of the combined Allied armies land on five Normandy beaches. Four beaches are taken easily but U.S. troops meet stiff German resistance at "Bloody Omaha." By nightfall, however, all five landing areas have been secured and Allied troops are pouring ashore. The campaign to defeat Germany is underway.

MAY 9, Crimea

The Crimean peninsula is cleared of German forces and the Soviets recapture Sevastopol. The Germans lose 100,000 men; Hitler blames Erich von Manstein, whom he dismisses from command of Army Group South.

JUNE 23, Belorussia

The Soviets launch their summer offensive. The Red Army has more than one and a quarter million men; the Germans number 500,000. The Soviets smash through the German lines, advancing 150 miles (240 km) in a week.

EYEWITNESS: Heinz Geyr, Omaha Beach, D-Day

"On June 6, we saw the full might of the English and Americans. At sea close in shore the fleet was drawn up, limitless ships small and great. No one who did not see it could have believed it. The whistling of the shells and shattering explosions created the worst kind of music. Our unit has suffered terribly; only a tiny handful of our company remains."

Poorly-armed soldiers of the Polish Home Army prepare for action.

Bridgehead – a small area secured in enemy territory.

German generals study a map as they try to defend northern France.

JULY 20, Belorussia

The city of Minsk falls to the Soviet advance; Army Group Center is totally destroyed. German losses exceed 200,000.

JULY 20, Germany

Hitler moves to his East Prussian HQ at Rastenburg. Colonel Count Claus Schenk von Stauffenberg makes an unsuccessful assassination attempt on Hitler, by placing a bomb in a briefcase in a conference room. Hitler is protected from the blast by the heavy table. Stauffenberg's fellow plotters fail to seize power in Berlin, as planned. He and the other conspirators are rounded up and executed.

JULY 20, Normandy

The American, British, and Canadian forces have consolidated their D-Day beachheads and link up to move southeast.

AUGUST 1, Poland

The Polish resistance—the "Home Army"—rises in Warsaw as the Soviets approach. Some 50,000 fighters retake most of the city before the Germans send in reinforcements and attack them for the next nine weeks. The Soviets refuse to help, or even to let the western Allies use Soviet airbases to send in supplies. The Home Army surrenders on October 2.

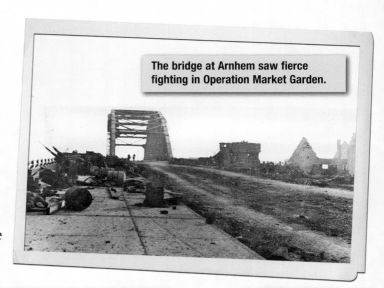

The bridge at Arnhem saw fierce fighting in Operation Market Garden.

EYEWITNESS: Alfred Molter, letter to his wife, July Bomb Plot

"Darling, have you heard the news about the attempt to assassinate the Leader? I had the feeling I just had to run somewhere and pray. Thank heavens that the Leader has been preserved for us. If the Leader was killed, then the war would be lost, and Goring would surely be killed as well. And that's what the bandits were looking to achieve. What venal pigs must have raised his hand to do this?"

Venal – able to betray one's principles in return for money.

TURNING POINTS: Ardennes Offensive

The Ardennes Offensive, or the Battle of the Bulge, began on December 16, 1944. The Germans launched a massive offensive through the hilly and wooded Ardennes region of southern Belgium in a last-ditch attempt to reverse the course of the war. Hitler hoped to get to Antwerp and split the Allied armies. While Allied aircraft were grounded by bad weather, the Fifth and Sixth Panzer Armies launched parallel attacks. The Fifth Army bypassed Bastogne, which the U.S. 101st Airborne Division held throughout the offensive, and advanced to the Meuse River. But the German troops were outnumbered, and fighting around Bastogne proved decisive. Having committed his last reserves, Hitler had nothing to fall back on. Allied victory was inevitable.

AUGUST 19, Baltic

Russian troops surround 55 German divisions on the Baltic coast. The Red Army enters Bucharest.

AUGUST 19, France

The Allies have now landed 1.5 million soldiers and 300,000 vehicles in France. They are better equipped than their German opponents. American troops advance through France from both the north and south. In Paris, the French resistance takes over part of the city.

SEPTEMBER 17, Holland

Operation Market Garden begins. This is General Montgomery's plan for an armored and airborne thrust through Holland. Meanwhile the new Allied supreme commander, General Dwight D. Eisenhower, decides on a broad advance toward the Rhine River. Allied forces now have a complete front stretching from the Channel to Switzerland; they advance toward the German West Wall, the Siegfried Line. France is now almost totally liberated.

NOVEMBER 12, Norway

The German battleship *Tirpitz* sinks at her anchorage when she is hit by a force of British Lancaster bombers.

DECEMBER 16, Ardennes

The Ardennes Offensive is launched in bad weather in the hills of southern Belgium. Hitler plans to reach Antwerp and split the Allied armies in the West. The operation is a gamble: Germany's last reserves of men and tanks have been committed to the offensive.

U.S. soldiers stand on antitank defenses in the German Siegfried Line.

EYEWITNESS: F. Werner, 12th Panzer Division, April 1945

"Some will regard the war in these critical days as lost. But the war is only lost if we surrender. Even should Germany capitulate, would the war be over for us? No, the horror would be only just really beginning and we would not even have weapons to defend ourselves. As long as we have weapons and the firm belief in our good cause, nothing is lost."

Bombs fall on Dresden on February 14. More than 50,000 people died.

JANUARY 3, Ardennes

The U.S. 101st Airborne are surrounded in the town of Bastogne. When they fight off a final German attack, Hitler's last offensive in the West has been stopped. The Allies regroup and launch a counterattack.

JANUARY 27, Poland

The Soviets liberate Auschwitz, the Third Reich's main death camp (in fact, the complex includes three separate camps). Between 1.1 and 1.5 million people died at Auschwitz; 90 percent of them were Jews. Other victims included a large number of Gypsies. Russian army groups take Warsaw and cross the river Oder within 100 miles (160 km) of Berlin. They reach the Baltic at Danzig and take industrial Silesia, and, with it, the last coal supplies of the Third Reich. Hitler responds to the Soviet offensive in the East by moving troops from the West to face it.

JANUARY 27, France

German losses since D-Day stand at 1.5 million, over half of which are prisoners of war.

FEBRUARY 14, East Prussia

The Kriegsmarine evacuates German troops (from Baltic ports, Danzig, and East Prussia) who have been trapped by the advance of the Red Army.

The bridge at Remagen was captured when demolition charges failed to go off.

Regroup – to gather and reorganize one's forces.

TURNING POINTS: The liberation of Auschwitz

On January 27, 1945, during the conquest of Poland, Soviet troops liberated the death camp of Auschwitz. Nobody was prepared for what they found. There were, in fact, three camps. Auschwitz I was reserved for political prisoners. Auschwitz II, or Birkenau, was turned by the SS into a huge concentration camp and extermination complex. Birkenau contained four large bath houses in which prisoners were gassed to death. Auschwitz III became a slave labor-camp in May 1942. As prisoners arrived at the camp, they were divided up. The young and able were sent to work; children, their mothers, and the old and weak were gassed immediately. Thousands more were sent to the camp doctor, Josef Mengele, who carried out horrific experiments in the name of science.

FEBRUARY 14, Dresden

805 RAF bombers attack the city during the night. The raid causes a massive firestorm that kills 50,000 people. The Americans then bomb the city during the day.

MARCH 3, France

General Patton's Third Army approaches the River Rhine.

MARCH 6, Hungary

Hitler launches Operation Spring Awakening to secure the oilfields at Nagykanizsa and retake Budapest. The offensive soon starts to fail in the face of bad weather and Red Army resistance.

MARCH 7, Germany

Despite orders from Hitler that not a single Rhine bridge must fall into Allied hands, the U.S. First Army manages to capture an undamaged bridge at Remagen near Bonn shortly before it is blown up by the retreating Germans. In less than 24 hours, more than 8,000 troops with tanks and guns cross the Rhine.

MARCH 19, Germany

Hitler issues the so-called Nero Decree. It orders the destruction of all bridges, factories, and railroads. However, the order is ignored by his deputy, Albert Speer, who is already thinking about the recovery of Germany after its inevitable defeat.

MARCH 22, Germany

General Montgomery's Twenty-First Army Group crosses the Rhine to the north. It then moves across north Germany, heading for the city of Hamburg.

The last picture of Adolf Hitler was taken outside the bunker in Berlin.

Firestorm – a huge blaze with high temperatures and strong winds.

Montgomery (right) discusses the surrender with German officers.

APRIL 2, Germany

The U.S. First and Third Armies link up, completing the encirclement of the industrial Ruhr region. Hitler's Third Reich is now crumbling rapidly.

APRIL 13, Austria

The Red Army takes Vienna. Later in April, the British liberate the Belsen concentration camp, and Soviet and U.S. troops meet on the River Elbe.

APRIL 26, Berlin

The Red Army begins its final assault on the German capital. Hitler is in the city, hidden in his underground bunker. He orders his nonexistent troops to come to the city's aid. German forces are restricted to an area 10 miles (16 km) long and 3 miles (5 km) wide.

APRIL 28, Italy

Mussolini tries to escape to Switzerland but is captured and shot by guerrilla fighters.

APRIL 29/30, Berlin

As Berlin is engulfed in explosions and gunfire, Hitler marries his mistress Eva Braun in the bunker. He dictates a political testament, stating "I die with a happy heart, aware of the immeasurable deeds and achievements of our soldiers at the front," before shooting himself. Eva Braun takes poison.

EYEWITNESS: Erich Dethleffsen, German POW

"It is only a few months since the collapse. We haven't gained the distance in time, or in mind, to be able to judge, to some extent objectively, what was error, guilt and crime, or inexorable fate. We Germans are still too taken up with prejudice. But we are also ashamed that we let ourselves be led astray and misused and that we knew nothing."

A German POW reads about Hitler's death in a U.S. forces newspaper.

POW – an abbreviation meaning prisoner of war.

TURNING POINTS: The death of Adolf Hitler

With an Allied victory assured, Hitler moved to his Führerbunker in Berlin in April 1945. The bunker was an underground complex of around 30 rooms some 50 feet (15 m) beneath the Chancellery Building. From there, he continued to direct his failed war effort. As the Soviets moved ever closer to the heart of Berlin and the city was engulfed in explosions and fires, Hitler married his long-term mistress, Eva Braun, on April 29. The following day, both he and his new wife committed suicide. Eva Braun took poison and Hitler shot himself. As Soviet shells exploded close by, the bodies were carried up to the Chancellery garden. Gasoline was poured over them and then they were set alight. The charred remains were then buried in a shell crater.

MAY 1, Berlin

Grand Admiral Karl Dönitz, the new head of state, orders his forces to maintain their discipline, but realizes that resistance to the Allies is useless.

MAY 2, Italy

Following negotiations between General Karl Wolff, governor of north Italy, and U.S. agent Allen Dulles of the Office of Strategic Service (OSS) in Switzerland to spare Italy from further destruction, Kesselring surrenders German forces in Italy.

MAY 4, Germany

Dönitz authorizes Admiral Friedeburg, head of the Kriegsmarine, to negotiate a separate but partial surrender to Field Marshal Montgomery of all German forces in northern Germany. This includes all German forces in Holland, northwest Germany including the Friesian Islands, Heligoland, and all other islands. The unconditional surrender takes effect at 8:30 a.m. the following morning, when German forces lay down their arms.

MAY 5, Germany

Friedeburg and Jodl fly to Eisenhower's headquarters in Rheims to negotiate the surrender of all remaining German forces in southern Germany and France.

MAY 10, Czechoslovakia

The Red Army liberates Prague. World War II is over. Germany is in ruins, and 500,000 citizens of the Third Reich have died in six years of war.

Berlin was left in ruins after the fighting in May 1945.

Glossary

accords Compromises between conflicting views.

amphibious Describes an operation that lands troops ashore from the sea.

annex To incorporate territory into an existing country.

Aryan In Nazi belief, a white member of a Nordic super race.

axis An alliance between countries to promote their shared interests.

Blitzkrieg German for "lightning war;" a tactic based on a rapid advance.

bridgehead A small area secured in enemy territory.

cede To give up or surrender territory.

chief of staff The most senior officer of an armed force.

coalition A government in which power is shared between parties.

commandos Soldiers who are specially trained to operate in small groups.

commissars Soviet personnel who educated troops in Communist ideology.

conscripts Soldiers who are forced to serve in the military.

convoy A group of merchant ships traveling together, protected by warships.

decree An order that has the same force as a law.

directive An order or instruction issued by a central authority.

euthanasia A policy of deliberately killing "unproductive" individuals.

firestorm A huge blaze with high temperatures and strong winds.

ghetto Part of a city where a particular ethnic group is forced to live, because of discrimination.

mobilization An order to a country's armed forces to make ready for war.

outflank To pass around the side of an enemy force.

pact A formal agreement between nations.

plebiscite A vote in which a population accepts or rejects a proposal.

pogrom The organized, often official, persecution of a minority, such as Jews.

propaganda Material intended to influence public opinion.

puppet state A government that carries out the wishes of the government of another country.

purge An operation to get rid of people who are seen as undesirable.

requisition To seize private property for official use.

retaliated Struck back in reaction to an act of violence.

scuttle To deliberately sink a ship to prevent it being captured.

siege A military operation in which a town or position is cut off.

strategic Related to the overall aims of a campaign, not to immediate results.

treason A crime intended to weaken or overthrow a government.

ultimatum A demand that, if it is not met, will lead to war.

venal Able to betray one's principles in return for money.

Further resources

Books

Ailsby, Christopher. *The Third Reich Day by Day*. Chartwell Books Inc, 2011.

Altman, Linda Jacobs. *Adolf Hitler: Evil Mastermind of the Holocaust* (Holocaust Heroes and Nazi Criminals). Enslow Publishers, 2005.

Altman, Linda Jacobs. *Hitler's Rise to Power and the Holocaust* (The Holocaust in History). Enslow Publishers, 2003.

Corrigan, Jim. *Causes of World War II* (The Road to War: Causes of Conflict). OTTN Publishing, 2005.

Dowswell, Paul. *The Causes of World War II*. Heinemann-Raintree, 2008.

Fitzgerald, Stephanie. *Kristallnacht, The Night of Broken Glass: Igniting the Nazi War Against Jews* (Snapshots in History). Compass Point Books, 2008.

Freeman, Charles. *Why Did the Rise of the Nazis Happen?* (Moments in History). Gareth Stevens Publishing, 2010.

Gogerly, Liz. *Adolf Hitler: From Failed Artist to Fascist Dictator* (Twentieth-Century History Makers). Raintree, 2003.

Hook, Sue Vander. *Adolf Hitler* (Essential Lives). Abdo Publishing Company, 2011.

Hynson, Colin. *World War II: A Primary Source History* (In Their Own Words). Gareth Stevens Publishing, 2005.

Rice, Earle. *Adolf Hitler and Nazi Germany* (World Leaders). Morgan Reynolds Publishing, 2005.

Worth, Richard. *Heinrich Himmler: Murderous Architect of the Holocaust* (Holocaust Heroes and Nazi Criminals). Enslow Publishers, 2005.

Websites

http://www.time.com/time/photogallery/0,29307,1707887,00.html
Time Magazine photo-essay charting Hitler's rise to power.

http://www.schoolhistory.co.uk/lessons/riseofhitler/
SchoolHistory.co.uk lesson about the reasons why Hitler was able to come to power.

http://www.historylearningsite.co.uk/Nazi Germany.htm
History Learning Site index to pages about all aspects of life in Nazi Germany.

http://www.johndclare.net/Weimar1.htm
John D. Clare's revision pages about Germany from 1919 to 1939.

http://www.bbc.co.uk/learningzone/clips/nazi-germany-opposing-views/3272.html
Video from the BCC of an American woman recalling life in Nazi Germany.

Index

For Every
Individual...

Renew by Phone
269-5222

Renew on the Web
www.indypl.org

For General Library Information
please call 275-4100